First Facts™

Water All Around

Water and the Weather

by Rebecca Olien

Consultant:
Peter R. Jaffé, Professor
Department of Civil and Environmental Engineering
Princeton University
Princeton, New Jersey

Capstone press
Mankato, Minnesota

First Facts is published by Capstone Press,
151 Good Counsel Drive, P.O. Box 669, Mankato, Minnesota 56002.
www.capstonepress.com

Library of Congress Cataloging-in-Publication Data
Olien, Rebecca.
    Water and the weather / by Rebecca Olien.
    p. cm.—(First facts. Water all around)
    Includes bibliographical references and index.
    ISBN 0-7368-3702-7 (hardcover)
    1. Weather—Juvenile literature. 2. Water—Juvenile literature. I. Title. II. Series.
QC981.3.O45 2005
551.5—dc22   2004011300

Summary: Explains how weather affects the water cycle, and how water forms rain, hail, snow,
    and sleet.

Editorial Credits
Christine Peterson, editor; Linda Clavel, designer; Ted Williams, illustrator; Kelly Garvin,
    photo researcher; Scott Thoms, photo editor

Photo Credits
Bruce Coleman Inc./CC Lockwood, 15; RJ Photo, 14
Corbis/Bruce Burkhardt, 19
IDRC/S. Mukerji, 20
Index Stock Imagery/Joseph Hancock, 5
Photodisc, 10
Richard Hamilton Smith, 16, 17
Tom Stack & Associates Inc./Doug Sokell, 12–13
Unicorn Stock Photos/Brenda Matthiesen, 6–7
Visuals Unlimited/Barbara K. Hesse, cover

Table of Contents

Changing Weather

Water is part of the weather. Water rises into the air as a gas called **vapor**. It forms clouds in the sky. Rain falls from clouds. On cold days, water falls to the earth as snow. Water makes the weather different every day.

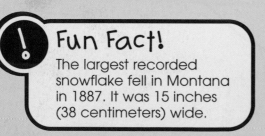

! Fun Fact!
The largest recorded snowflake fell in Montana in 1887. It was 15 inches (38 centimeters) wide.

The Water Cycle

Water changes forms in the water cycle. The sun's heat turns liquid water into vapor. Vapor rises into the air. It cools to form clouds. Rain or snow falls from clouds to fill oceans, lakes, and rivers. The water cycle never ends.

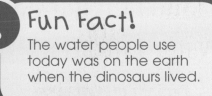

Fun Fact!
The water people use today was on the earth when the dinosaurs lived.

Currents Cause Weather

Currents push warm and cold air around the planet. Weather changes when warm and cold air currents meet.

Air currents pull vapor from water. The warm vapor rises into the air. It cools to form clouds. Clouds fill with water. Water falls to the earth as **precipitation**.

Water vapor

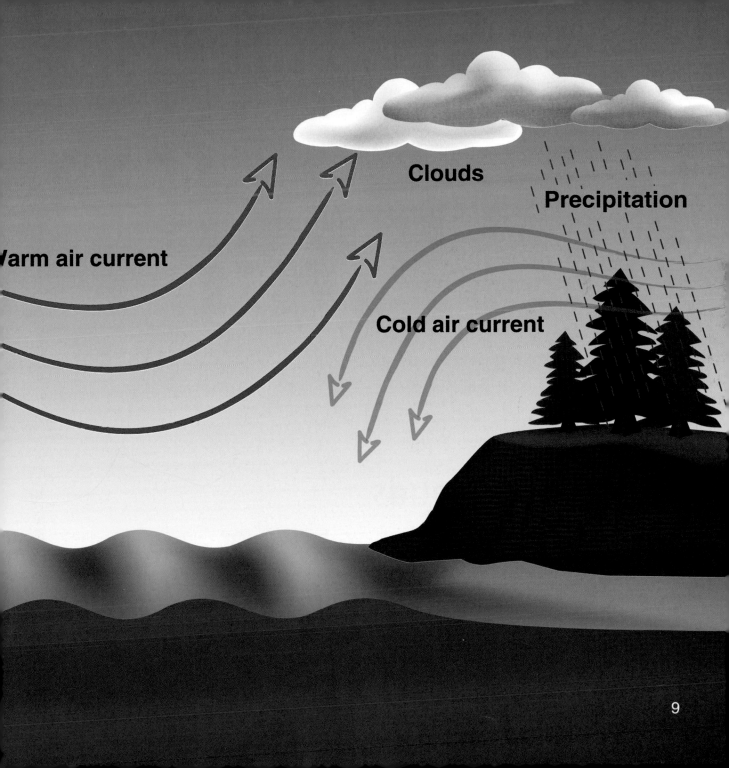

Warm air current

Clouds

Precipitation

Cold air current

Types of Clouds

Clouds form when water vapor turns into tiny drops. Vapor **condenses** on tiny bits of dust. Millions of drops stick together to form a cloud.

Three main kinds of clouds fill the sky. **Cirrus** clouds are thin and light. **Cumulus** clouds look fluffy and white. **Stratus** clouds are gray and flat.

Cirrus

Cumulus

Stratus

Clouds Fill with Water

Clouds hold water that turns to rain or snow. Water drops rise and fall inside clouds. They make bigger drops. Clouds grow dark as they fill with water.

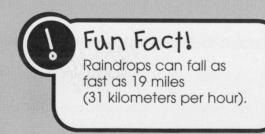

Fun Fact!
Raindrops can fall as fast as 19 miles (31 kilometers per hour).

Rain and Hail

Most water falls to the earth as rain. Water drops get bigger as more water condenses. Drops become too heavy to stay in the air. They fall as rain.

Hail is ice that falls from the sky. Cold air high in the clouds turns water drops to ice. Hail gets heavy and falls from the clouds.

Snow and Sleet

Snow forms as ice crystals in clouds. Water freezes when the temperature is below 32 degrees Fahrenheit (0 degrees Celsius). Heavy snow falls from clouds.

Sleet is rain that freezes as it falls
to the earth. Raindrops fall from clouds.
The drops pass through cold air. The
drops freeze into small bits of ice.

Weather Returns Water

Weather returns water to the earth. Clouds grow dark as they fill with water. Precipitation falls from clouds as rain, hail, snow, or sleet. Precipitation fills oceans, lakes, and rivers. Weather keeps water flowing on the earth.

 Fun Fact!

An average cumulus cloud weighs about the same as six army tanks.

Amazing but True!

People in Chungungo, Chile, catch clouds for water. The town gets only a few inches of rain each year. Nets catch fog floating over the hills. Water condenses on the nets and drips into pipes. The nets catch about 2,500 gallons (9,500 liters) of water a day. People use the water for drinking, cooking, and washing.

Hands On: Sticky Drops

Big drops of water are made of smaller drops. Water drops inside a cloud also stick together. They get bigger and heavier until they fall to the ground as rain. Try this activity to see how drops of water stick together.

What You Need

water
waxed paper
plate
straw

What You Do

1. Sprinkle a few drops of water on a piece of waxed paper.
2. Hold up one end of the waxed paper over a plate. Watch how fast the drops run down the paper.
3. Sprinkle water drops on another piece of waxed paper.
4. Keep the paper flat. Blow gently through the straw to move the drops together.
5. Blow the drops together so there are only a few big drops on the paper.
6. Hold up one end of the paper. Watch how much faster the large drops run down the paper.

Glossary

cirrus (SIHR-uhss)—high, feathery white cloud

condense (kuhn-DENSS)—to change from gas to liquid; water vapor condenses into liquid water.

cumulus (KYOO-muh-luhss)—puffy cloud

current (KUR-uhnt)—the movement of air in a certain direction

hail (HAYL)—balls of ice that form in clouds and fall to the ground

precipitation (pri-sip-i-TAY-shuhn)—water that falls from clouds to the earth's surface in the form of rain, snow, sleet, or hail

sleet (SLEET)—tiny particles of ice that fall from clouds

stratus (STRAH-tuhss)—layered cloud

vapor (VAY-pur)—a gas made from a liquid

Read More

Adams, Simon. *The Best Book of Weather.* New York: Kingfisher, 2001.

Sherman, Josepha. *Splish, Splash!: A Book About Rain.* Amazing Science. Minneapolis: Picture Window Books, 2004.

Internet Sites

FactHound offers a safe, fun way to find Internet sites related to this book. All of the sites on FactHound have been researched by our staff.

Here's how:
1. Visit *www.facthound.com*
2. Type in this special code **0736837027** for age-appropriate sites. Or enter a search word related to this book for a more general search.
3. Click on the **Fetch It** button.

FactHound will fetch the best sites for you!

Index

cirrus, 11

clouds, 4, 7, 8, 10–11, 12, 15,
     16, 17, 18, 20

condensation, 10, 14, 20

cumulus, 11, 18

currents, 8

earth, 4, 7, 8, 14, 17, 18

fog nets, 20

hail, 15, 18

ice, 15, 16, 17

lakes, 7, 18

oceans, 7, 18

precipitation, 8, 18

rain, 4, 7, 12, 14, 17, 18, 20

rivers, 7, 18

sleet, 17, 18

snow, 4, 7, 12, 16, 18

stratus, 11

vapor, 4, 7, 8, 10

water cycle, 7